Hot Air Balloons

by Kris Bonnell

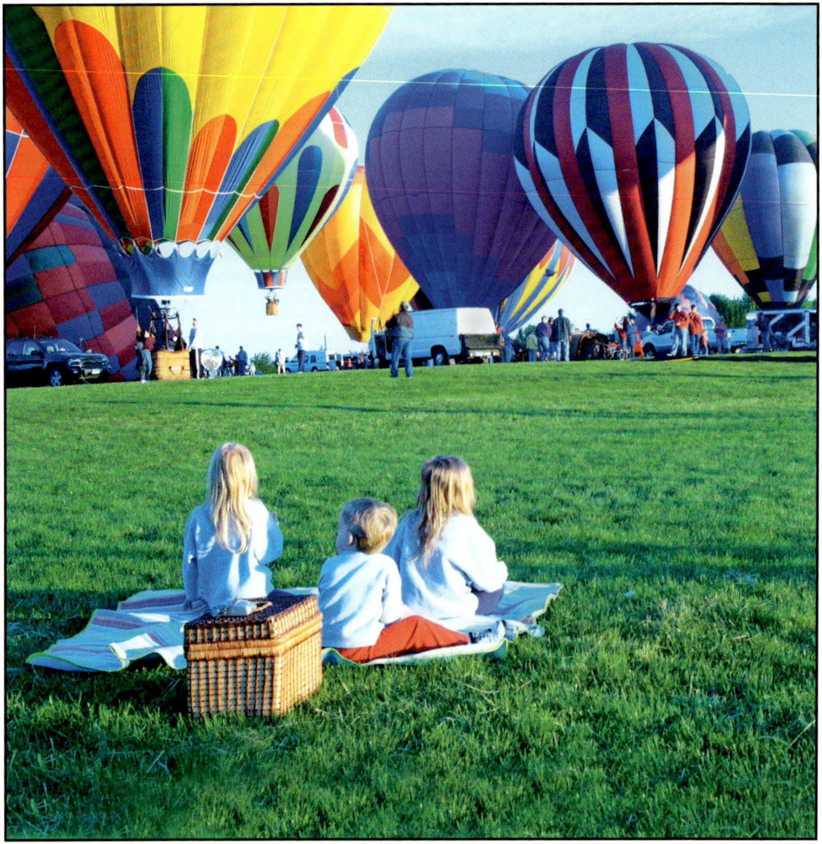

Hot air balloons
are big balloons
that we can ride in.

The top of a hot air balloon is called the bag.

We ride in the basket.

This hot air balloon is going to go up.

This balloon is going up.

Hot air going into the bag makes the balloon go up.

9

A hot air balloon can go way up into the sky.
It can go over the trees.

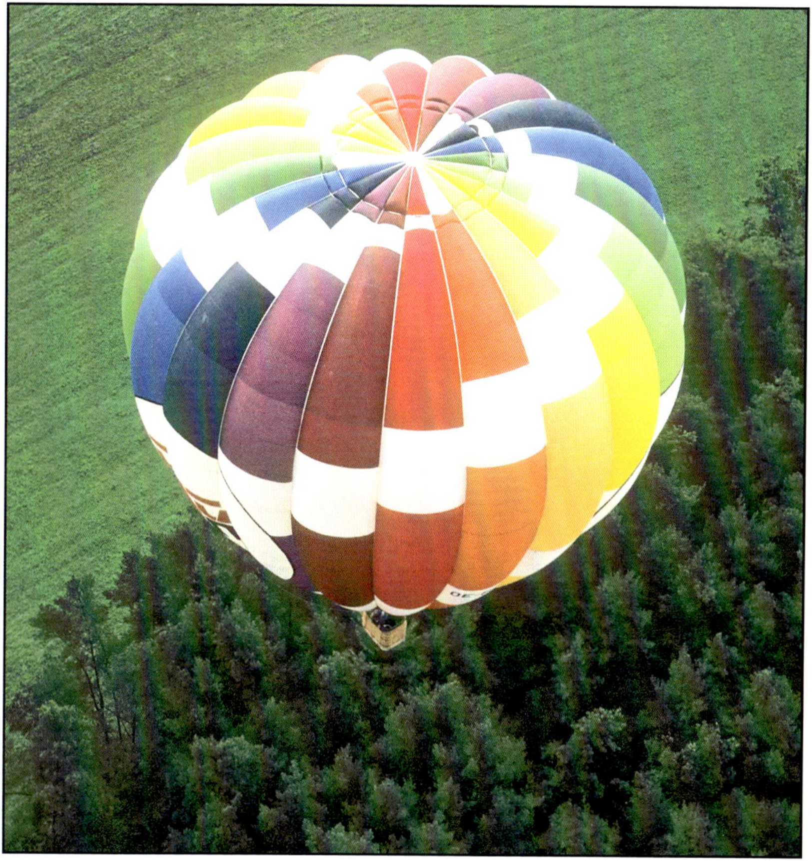

A balloon comes down when the air inside the bag is not hot.

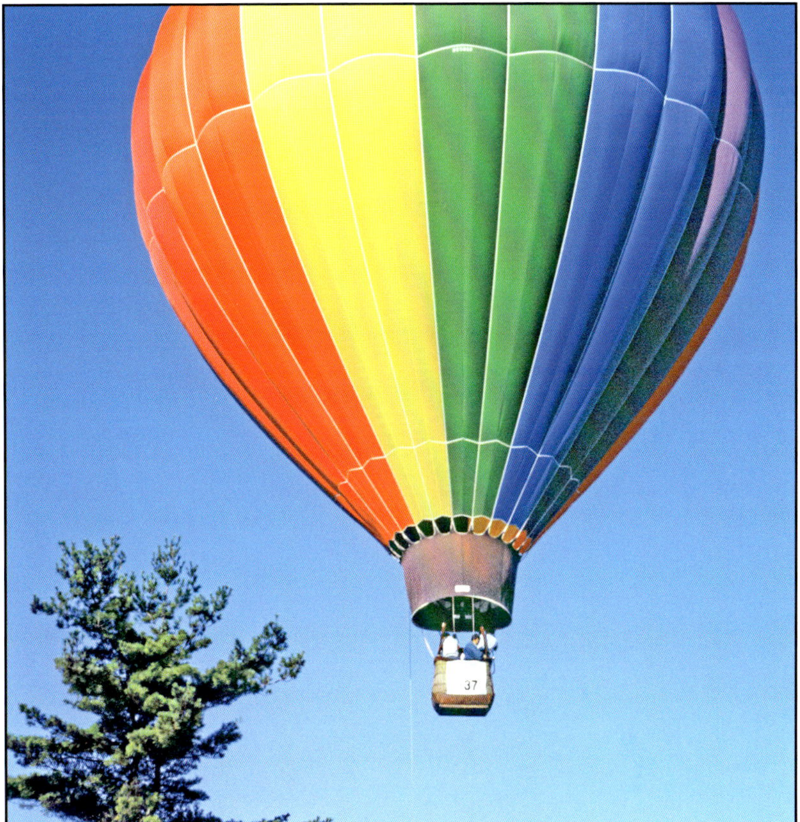
37

This balloon is down.
The air is coming out.
The ride is over.

15

Hot Air Balloon Words

bag

basket